Wh
Hell?

Basics of the Faith

What Is Hell?

Christopher W. Morgan & Robert A. Peterson

P&R PUBLISHING
P.O. BOX 817 • PHILLIPSBURG • NEW JERSEY 08865-0817

Scripture quotations are from *ESV Bible* ® (*The Holy Bible, English Standard Version* ®). Copyright © 2001 by Crossway Bibles, a publishing ministry of Good News Publishers. Used by permission. All rights reserved.

Page design by Tobias Design

Printed in the United States of America

Library of Congress Cataloging-in-Publication Data

Morgan, Christopher W., 1971-
  What is hell? / Christopher W. Morgan and Robert A. Peterson.
    p. cm. - - (Basics of the faith)
  Includes bibliographical references.
  ISBN 978-1-59638-199-5 (pbk.)
  1. Hell--Christianity. I. Peterson, Robert A., 1948- II. Title.
  BT836.3.M67 2010
  236'.25--dc22

                              2010006411

◻ On October 24, 2003, the *Los Angeles Times* ran an article called "Next Stop, the Pearly Gates or Hell?" It reported a survey conducted by the Barna Research Group. The September 2003 survey polled people from every state but Hawaii and Alaska to discover their beliefs about heaven and hell. The poll found that 76 percent of Americans believe in a heaven and that 71 percent believe in a hell.[1] The results were a bit surprising: according to the poll, almost as many Americans said they believe in hell as in heaven. But more telling was the fact that, although more than seven out of ten Americans believe in some sort of hell, fewer than one out of a hundred think they have a good chance of going there!

These findings are similar to those described in a 1991 cover story of *U.S. News & World Report*. Its 1990 poll found that 60 percent of Americans said they believed in some sort of hell, but that only 4 percent considered themselves to have a good chance of going there.[2]

What are we to make of this? Polls are difficult to analyze, but if these are accurate, more Americans believed in hell in 2003 than in 1990. Yet fewer of them believed that they themselves might go to hell. Evidently, most Americans conclude that God will punish at least some sinners, but few include themselves in that group. Maybe the idea is that hell exists only for extremely evil people—such as Adolf Hitler, Saddam Hussein, serial killers, and serial rapists.

These ideas are echoed in a question we have often been asked: would a loving God really send good people to hell? Maybe you have been asked that question. It troubles non-Christians as well as Christians, even pastors, missionaries, elders, deacons, and teachers. Pastor and author Tim Keller considers it one of the major questions that contemporary Christians face when they share the gospel.[3]

Would a loving God really send good people to hell? What does the Bible teach? It is important to remember that the Bible is the Word of God and is therefore true (2 Tim. 3:14–17; 2 Peter 1:20–21). Indeed, the Bible speaks truth, even when it says things we may not like. It is crucial that we hold to this. Otherwise, we may believe whatever we want to believe, rather than that which is actually true. For example, we may both want the St. Louis Cardinals to win the World Series every year, but the truth of the matter is that they win only occasionally (though more than most!). What we want to believe must come to terms with what is. And Christians throughout the centuries have known that whatever the Bible teaches on a subject is true, whether they like its particular teachings or not. We must deliberately and consistently submit our thoughts, wills, and emotions to the clear teaching of Scripture.

WOULD A LOVING GOD REALLY SEND GOOD PEOPLE TO HELL?

With that in mind, what does the Bible teach regarding this crucial question? It says a lot, as Paul's letter to the Romans demonstrates. From the outset of the letter, Paul asserts that he is "not ashamed of the gospel, for it is the power of God for salvation" (1:16). It is the only way anyone—Jew or Gentile alike—is saved. All need the gospel.[4]

Paul then points out why. Romans 1:18–32 makes clear that through his creation, God shows himself to be the powerful Creator, the One alone deserving worship from all, including those without the Bible. But people do not worship God as they should. Instead we all reject him. We "suppress" or resist the truth and trade in God for idols. Though we are made by God and for him (see also Col. 1:16), we make life all about ourselves. This is idolatry, a sort of cosmic treason. What does God do about this? He judges us guilty and sets his wrath upon us.

In Romans 2 and 3, Paul continues to show that all are guilty before God. Moral people are guilty because they fail to live up to the standards that they place on others (2:1–11). Even religious people, such as the Jews, are guilty. They have the law but break it and show themselves to be sinners before God (2:12–3:8). Paul sums up his argument: all, both Jews and Gentiles, are under sin (3:9). There are no exceptions. He quotes a litany of Old Testament passages to show that no one is righteous, no one understands, no one seeks for God, everyone has turned aside, no one does good, no one fears God (3:10–18).

The apostle then concludes that, based on performance, no human being can stand before God as righteous. Rather, all are sinners who refuse to love, worship, and obey God as he deserves. Indeed, sin infects our minds—we do not think correctly about God. Sin infects our desires—we do not want what we know we should want, and we want what we know we should not want. Sin infects our choices—we choose wrongly because we want something else more than God. Human sin is universal and total.

Elsewhere, Paul stresses that we are all "by nature children of wrath, like the rest of mankind" (Eph. 2:3). We are in

Adam's fall, united in his sin and guilt (Rom. 5:12–21). And we all also stumble in many ways. In other words, we are sinful by nature and choice and are under God's just judgment.

Many in our culture suppose that at the final judgment God will use measuring scales. If our good deeds outweigh our bad ones, then we will make it into heaven. If others' bad deeds outweigh their good ones, they will go to hell. But in Romans Paul paints a different picture. He teaches that we are *all* guilty (3:9–20, 23), and that our guilt is enormous and increasing (2:5). And there is nothing we can do to remove this guilt (3:19–20).

Thankfully, Paul does not end here, but reveals that although we cannot be justified by our own deeds, we can be declared right with God on account of Jesus' saving work (3:21–31). His work, centered here in his substitutionary death on the cross, displays God's love and justice. It shows that God loves us, even while we were sinners (see also 5:6–11). And it shows that God is just, requiring that the penalty of our sin and guilt be paid (3:24–26). But instead of our paying the penalty, Jesus voluntarily takes it upon himself. All who have faith in Jesus will be declared right with God because their sin has been transferred to Christ's spiritual bank account (3:21–5:11). All others will suffer the consequence of their sin and guilt, which is hell.

It is important to note here that the question Paul struggles to answer is not the modern one: "Would a loving God really send good people to hell?" Instead, Paul addresses this: "How could a just and holy God ever declare guilty sinners to be righteous in his sight?" The contours of Paul's answer are that we are all sinners and therefore all guilty, and our just punishment is hell. Most importantly, only Jesus' saving work—his death and resurrection—can atone for sins. And not only is Christ the only way to be forgiven of our guilt, but only faith in Christ can bring that forgiveness. Paul develops these ideas in Romans 4–5. We are ungodly sinners and enemies of God (5:6–10), and only Christ and faith in him make us right before God (5:9–10, 18–19; 4:1–25).

Paul is not the only one to emphasize these truths. John 3:36 states, "Whoever believes in the Son has eternal life; whoever does not obey the Son shall not see life, but the wrath of God remains on him." Jesus says, "I am the way, and the truth, and the life. No one comes to the Father except through me" (John 14:6). In Acts 4:12, Peter and John proclaim, "And there is salvation in no one else, for there is no other name under heaven given among men by which we must be saved." Peter confesses, "Christ also suffered once for sins, the righteous for the unrighteous, that he might bring us to God" (1 Peter 3:18).

So would a loving God really send good people to hell? We can now say that this is a loaded question! It is distorted in three ways. First, God is defined only in terms of love. Certainly, God is more loving than any of us can comprehend (Eph. 3:14–19). God is not less than loving; he is more than loving. He is also holy, just, and good. His wrath toward sin is just and is a proper display of his holiness and goodness. A good and just judge punishes the guilty (Rom. 1:18–3:10).

The second distortion is that people are described as "good" in the question. Paul makes it clear that "no one" is righteous, good, or reverent toward God (Rom. 3:9–20), "not even one" (3:12). Rather, "all have sinned and fall short of the glory of God" (3:23).

Third, the question also distorts the portrait of God by portraying him as the one sending people to hell, as if he happily does so. But Paul puts the blame squarely on our shoulders. We are rebels who deserve the punishment of our sins, which is hell. Sinners have only themselves to blame.

"Would a loving God really send good people to hell?" is the wrong question, and it leads people to wrong answers. The right question, the one that Paul answers in Romans, is, "How can a loving and just God declare the guilty to be right with him?" Or: "How can those who deserve hell go to heaven?" Because of Adam's sin and our own many sins, God could justly send us all to hell. Astonishingly, because of his grace alone, God loves us so much that he sent Jesus to die in our place and rise again to save us. And Jesus loves us so much that he did this willingly. And the Holy Spirit loves us so much that he opens our hearts to the gospel. And all those who trust the Lord Jesus as Savior will be declared right with God and their sins will be forgiven. And if you have not done so, we urge you to despair of saving yourself and to put your confidence in Christ, whose death and resurrection alone rescue the lost. All others will pay the penalty of their sins in hell.

Now that we have seen how hell fits into the larger gospel message, we can look more particularly at what the Bible teaches about the fate of the lost.

WHAT DOES THE BIBLE TEACH ABOUT HELL?

The Bible teaches much about hell, but five truths predominate.

Hell Is Punishment

Hell is a place where people suffer the just penalty for their moral crimes. Punishment is the Bible's primary picture of hell. That hell is punishment is clearly communicated by every New Testament author: Matthew (5:20–30; 24–25); Mark (9:42–48); Luke (16:19–31); Paul (2 Thess. 1:5–10); the author of Hebrews (10:27–31); James (4:12; 5:1–5); Peter (2 Peter 2:4–17); Jude (13–23); and John (Rev. 20:10–15). Three passages are most striking.

The first contains Jesus' startling words recorded in Matthew 25:31–46. This passage is well known for its emphasis on Jesus' solidarity with his people and the necessity of displaying faith through works of love. But it is also instructive about hell:

> When the Son of Man comes in his glory, and all the angels with him, then he will sit on his glorious throne. Before him will be gathered all the nations, and he will separate people one from another as a shepherd separates the sheep from the goats. And he will place the sheep on his right, but the goats on the left. Then the King will say to those on his right, "Come, you who are blessed by my Father, inherit the kingdom prepared for you from the foundation of the world." . . . Then the righteous will answer him, saying, "Lord, when did we see you hungry and feed you, or thirsty and give you drink? And when did we see you a stranger and welcome you, or naked and clothe you? And when did we see you sick or in prison and visit you?" And the King will answer them, "Truly, I say to you, as you did it to one of the least of these my brothers, you did it to me." Then he will say to those on his left, "Depart from me, you cursed, into the eternal fire prepared for the devil and his angels." . . . Then they also will answer, saying, "Lord, when did we see you hungry or thirsty or a stranger or naked or sick or in prison, and did not minister to you?" Then he will answer them, saying, "Truly, I say to you, as you did not do it to one of the least of these, you did not do it to me." And these will go away into eternal punishment, but the righteous into eternal life.

Jesus exercises the divine prerogative as judge to determine the eternal destinies of all. People's destinies are linked to their relationship to him, revealed in their treatment of his followers. He consigns the wicked to "eternal punishment" and grants the righteous "eternal life."

The second passage belongs to the apostle Paul, who encourages believers suffering at the hands of persecutors in 2 Thessalonians 1:5–10:

> This is evidence of the righteous judgment of God, that you may be considered worthy of the kingdom of God, for which you are also suffering—since indeed God considers it just to repay with affliction those who afflict you, and to grant relief to you who are afflicted as well as to us, when the Lord Jesus is revealed from heaven with his mighty angels in flaming fire, inflicting vengeance on those who do not know God and on those who do not obey the gospel of our Lord Jesus. They will suffer the punishment of eternal destruction, away from the presence of the Lord and from the glory of his might, when he comes on that day to be glorified in his saints, and to be marveled at among all who have believed, because our testimony to you was believed.

Notice how Paul comforts these believers by emphasizing God's just judgment: "The righteous judgment of God . . . God considers it just to repay with affliction those who afflict you . . . inflicting vengeance on those who do not know God and on those who do not obey the gospel of our Lord Jesus. They will suffer the punishment." God is the just judge who declares sinners guilty and punishes accordingly. Hell is appropriate retributive punishment on unbelievers.

Third, like Jesus and Paul, John also stresses that hell is just punishment. In Revelation 20:10–15, he recounts the final judgment and the appropriate punishment of the wicked:

> And the devil who had deceived them was thrown into the lake of fire and sulfur where the beast and the false prophet were, and they will be tormented day and night forever and ever. Then I saw a great white throne and him who was seated on it. From his presence earth and sky fled away, and no place was found for them. And I saw the dead, great and small, standing before the throne, and books were opened. Then another book was opened, which is the book of life. And the dead were judged by what was written in the books, according to what they had done. And the sea gave up the dead who were in it, Death and Hades gave up the dead who were in them, and they were judged, each one of them, according to what they had done. Then Death and Hades were thrown into the lake of fire. This is the second death, the lake of fire. And if anyone's name was not found written in the book of life, he was thrown into the lake of fire.

These three passages stress that, in the end, God's justice will prevail. The wicked are cast into hell, and the righteous experience the glorious presence of God on the new earth. The punishment of hell is deserved. It is just. The justice of the future punishment of the wicked is for the most part assumed by the biblical writers—a just God judges justly. Yet for clarity and emphasis, the biblical writers sometimes stress the justice of the retributive punishment.

It is important to see that the biblical writers underscore the justice of hell in order to comfort persecuted believers. Indeed, we could speak of the "comfort of hell." This is ironic because the doctrine of hell leads many today to question the justice of God. In the early church, however, hell reassured God's people that ultimately evil and evildoers would be defeated. God will one day conquer everything opposed to him and bring total victory, justice, and peace. Everyone on God's side will share in his victory; everyone opposing him and his people will be brought down (see also Luke 16:19–31; 2 Thess. 1:5–10; James 1:9–11; Rev. 6:10; 11:15–18; 14:14–15:4; 19:1–8; 20–22). When God's people are oppressed in the current evil age, these truths are not disturbing. Rather, they are the very ground of hope. These truths enable believers to endure suffering with the confidence that God will ultimately win and that they will reign with him.

Hell Is Destruction

Second, hell as destruction or death also plays a central role in Scripture. This theme occurs in the writings of most New Testament authors. The only exception is Mark, who addresses hell in just one passage, so it is not surprising that he does not allude to hell as the destruction of human beings. Destruction is clearly used as a depiction of hell in Matthew 7:13–14, 24–27; 24:51; Luke 13:3–5; John 3:16; Romans 9:22; Philippians 1:28; 3:19; 1 Thessalonians 5:3; 2 Thessalonians 1:5–10; 1 Timothy 6:9; Hebrews 10:27; James 1:11, 15; 4:12; 5:3–5, 20; 2 Peter 2:6; and Revelation 21:8.

Jesus speaks of destruction as the future of unbelievers: "Enter by the narrow gate. For the gate is wide and the way is easy that leads to destruction, and those who enter by it are many. For the gate is narrow and the way is hard that leads to life, and those who find it are few" (Matt. 7:13–14).

The apostle John also contrasts the final states in terms of life and death: "For God so loved the world, that he gave his only Son, that whoever believes in him should not perish but have eternal life" (John 3:16). Those who believe in Christ have eternal life, and those who do not will perish. Later in Revelation 20:14 and 21:8, John speaks of future punishment of the wicked as "the second death."

And as noted previously, Paul in 2 Thessalonians 1:5–10 teaches about hell not only as punishment but also as destruction, even calling it "eternal destruction" (1:9). Paul also speaks of the future punishment of unbelievers in terms of death: "For the wages of sin is death, but the free gift of God is eternal life in Christ Jesus our Lord" (Rom. 6:23).

What does hell as destruction and death mean? Douglas Moo ably answers. *Destruction* and its related words in the New Testament "refer to the situation of a person or object that has lost the essence of its nature or function." Moo notes that *destroy* and *destruction* can refer to barren land (Ezek. 6:14; 14:16), to ointment that is poured out wastefully (Matt. 26:8; Mark 14:4), to wineskins with holes that no longer function (Matt. 9:17; Mark 2:22; Luke 5:37), to a lost coin (Luke 15:9), or even to the entire world that "perished," that is, ceased to be an inhabited world, in the flood (2 Peter 3:6). Moo concludes, "In none of these cases do the objects cease to exist; they cease to be useful or to exist in their original, intended state."[5]

So hell is destruction in the sense that it is final and utter loss, ruin, or waste. This picture graphically illustrates that those in hell have failed to embrace the meaning of life and have wasted it. Trying to find life in themselves and sin, they forfeited true life. Only ruins remain.

Hell Is Banishment

A third key picture of hell in the New Testament is banishment. The idea of hell as banishment, separation, exclusion, or being left outside occurs in the writings of most New Testament authors. It does not, however, emerge in James or Hebrews.

Hell as banishment is prominent in the teachings of Jesus, particularly in the gospel of Matthew. This makes sense because kingdom themes are prominent in Jesus' teaching in Matthew. Jesus contrasts two future destinies: believers are welcomed into the kingdom while the wicked are banished from it.

Matthew records John the Baptist's preaching the final separation of the righteous from the wicked, noting that the wicked will be thrown into hell and burned "with unquench- able fire" (Matt. 3:1–12). Later Jesus proclaims that he will judge the world and declare to unbelievers, "Depart from me" (Matt. 7:21–23). In doing so, he personally excludes them from his kingdom. Jesus regularly portrays hell as being out- side the kingdom (and in outer darkness) and the wicked as shut out from God's kingdom (Matt. 8:12; 13:41–42, 49–50; 25:10–12, 30). In his sermon related to the end times (the Olivet Discourse), Jesus again shows that he will personally banish people from the kingdom. He exclaims to the wicked, "Depart from me, you cursed, into the eternal fire prepared for the devil and his angels" (Matt. 25:41).

Other gospel writers also depict this aspect of hell. Mark includes Jesus' teaching that the wicked are thrown into hell (Mark 9:42–48). Luke recounts the parable of the rich man and Lazarus, in which Jesus portrays the rich man in Hades as separated by a great chasm from Lazarus in heaven (Luke 16:19–31). John incorporates Jesus' warning about the Father's "taking away" fruitless branches from him (John 15:1–7).

Paul paints a stark picture of banishment in 2 Thes- salonians 1:5–10. There he teaches that those in hell will be "away from" Jesus' presence and glorious majesty (v. 9). In

Revelation 20–22, John shows what hell is like by contrasting it with heaven. In heaven, the saints will experience the glorious presence of God. But the wicked are left outside, unable to enter the heavenly city and forever excluded from wondrous fellowship with God (Rev. 22:14–15).

Whereas punishment stresses the justice of hell, banishment highlights what those in hell miss. Evangelicals often hint at this idea of banishment when they say that hell is eternal "separation from God." While the idea of separation is certainly correct and included in this New Testament concept of banishment, *separation* alone does not do justice to the force of this picture of hell. It is akin to using the phrase *passing away* as a euphemism for *death*. *Separation* from God could imply divine passivity, but *banishment* suggests God's active judgment. *Banishment* underscores the dreadfulness of exclusion from God's grace and stresses the desolation and finality of the predicament. Through this picture of hell, Scripture reveals that Christ eternally excludes the unrighteous from his kingdom. The wicked never experience fellowship with God. They are forever banished from his majestic presence and completely miss the reason for their existence—"to glorify God and to enjoy him forever" (Westminster Shorter Catechism no. 1).

Hell Is a Place of Suffering

Fourth, Scripture teaches that those in hell experience suffering. This is a frequent emphasis in the New Testament.

John the Baptist teaches that God will burn the wicked "with unquenchable fire" (Matt. 3:12). Jesus teaches that hell is a fate worse than being drowned in the sea (Mark 9:42). Indeed, it is worse than any earthly suffering—even being maimed (Matt. 5:29–30; Mark 9:43). Still worse, the suffering never ends (Matt. 25:41; Mark 9:48). Being cast into hell is likened to being thrown into a fiery furnace and means suffering unimaginable sorrow, remorse, and pain. The pain is described as "weeping and gnashing of teeth" (Matt. 8:12; 13:42, 50; 22:13; 24:51; 25:30). Moreover, it seems likely that this suffering is both emotional/spiritual and physical (involving bodily resurrection) (John 5:28–29).

The author of Hebrews warns that hell is utterly fearful and dreadful (Heb. 10:27–31). James depicts graphically the suffering linked to future punishment as "miseries that are coming" upon the wicked, eating their "flesh like fire" in "a day of slaughter" (5:1–5).

John's portraits in Revelation are hard to forget. Those in hell will feel the full force of God's fury (Rev. 14:10). They will "be tormented with fire" (14:10–11). This suffering is best understood as endless, since the "smoke of their torment goes up forever and ever" (14:11). Even worse, the suffering is constant. Those in hell will "have no rest, day or night" (14:11), and "will be tormented day and night forever and ever" (20:10).

Finally, this suffering is conscious. If hell did not consist of conscious suffering, it would be hard to see how it could in any meaningful sense be worse than death, be worse than earthly suffering, be filled with weeping and gnashing of teeth, or be a place of misery. These images communicate that people in hell will be aware that they are suffering just punishment.

Hell Is Eternal

Although this truth is very hard, the historic church has confessed that the suffering of the lost in hell will have no end.[6] This is contrary to universalism and annihilationism. Universalism is the view that in the end everyone will be gathered into the love of God and be saved. Because of the Bible's strong teaching on hell, universalism is held by few evangelicals. By contrast, annihilationism has gained adherents.[7] This view, also known as conditional immortality, or conditionalism for short, holds that the wicked will be cast into hell to suffer for their sins. When they have paid the debt for their sins, God will exterminate them so that they will exist no more.

We distinguish universalism and annihilationism, but oppose both of them because of Scripture's clear teaching that the punishment of hell is never-ending. We can only summarize here what we have previously explained in more detail.[8]

Daniel contrasts "everlasting life" with "shame and everlasting contempt" as fates of the resurrected righteous and unrighteous, respectively (Dan. 12:2). Along with "the new heavens and the new earth" for the righteous, Isaiah foresees this fate for "the dead bodies of the men who have rebelled against" God: "Their worm shall not die, their fire shall not be quenched" (Isa. 66:22, 24). Jesus appeals to this passage in Isaiah when he warns his hearers that going to hell means "unquenchable fire," a place "where their worm does not die and the fire is not quenched" (Mark 9:43, 48).

In the most famous passage on hell, Jesus equates the final fate of unsaved human beings with that of "the devil and his angels"—"eternal fire" (Matt. 25:41). Revelation 20:10 leaves no doubt as to that fate: "They will be tormented day and night forever and ever." Furthermore, five verses later in Matthew's gospel, Jesus contrasts the destinies of the goats and the sheep, describing them both as "eternal": "And these will go away into eternal punishment, but the righteous into eternal life" (Matt. 25:46). Jesus describes both destinies in a single sentence as "eternal."[9] Unless one is prepared to limit the bliss of the righteous, it is difficult to escape the conclusion that the punishment of the lost is also without end.

Jude speaks of a "punishment of eternal fire" and warns that false teachers are "wandering stars, for whom the gloom of utter darkness has been reserved forever" (Jude 7, 13).

Revelation 14 powerfully testifies to the eternity of hell. The idolater "will drink the wine of God's wrath, poured full strength into the cup of his anger, and he will be tormented with fire and sulfur. . . . And the smoke of their torment goes up forever" (vv. 10–11). Far from being annihilated, the lost "have no rest, day or night" (v. 11).

The endlessness of this punishment is also confirmed by the forceful pronouncement in Revelation 20:10, where it is said of Satan, among others: "The devil . . . was thrown into the lake of fire and sulfur . . . and they will be tormented day and night forever and ever." Five verses later John teaches, in agreement with Matthew 25:41, that unsaved human beings will share the devil's fate: "And if anyone's name was not found written in the book of life, he was thrown into the lake of fire" (Rev. 20:15).

Regardless of what we would like to be true, Scripture's witness is clear: the suffering of the wicked in body and soul in hell will never end. There will never come a time when people in hell find relief. They rebelled against God and missed out on true life forever. They are punished by God and banished from his kingdom, and they suffer endlessly. In rejecting God, they will never experience his glorious presence and the ultimate covenant blessing, which is eternal life. What a tragedy!

HOW DOES HELL AFFECT OUR THEOLOGY AND PRACTICE?

We are concerned that many who believe in hell do not realize its place in the Christian worldview. We are also concerned that many who believe the historic teaching about hell seem to keep the truth at arm's distance so that it does not significantly impact them. Because of this, we will address the relationship between the doctrine of hell and other central tenets in theology. And along the way, we will seek to address how our theology of hell should shape our lives.

Theological Faithfulness and Hell

Addressing the recent tensions over universalism and annihilationism, J. I. Packer acknowledges that evangelicals might wish that universalism were true. "No evangelical, I think, need hesitate to admit that in his heart of hearts he would like universalism to be true. Who can take pleasure in the thought of people being eternally lost? If you want to see folks damned, there is something wrong with you."[10] Nevertheless, Packer reminds us that the Bible closes the door on universal salvation and annihilationism.

Packer is right—it is difficult to come to terms with what the Word of God teaches about hell. It is difficult at times to submit our beliefs to the clear teaching of Scripture. That is why from the beginning, we emphasized that the Bible is true and that our beliefs must be based on the Bible, not on our thoughts, emotions, or cultural consensus. We do not want to think our friends and family deserve to be punished in hell. At times we wish God would just overlook our sin, but we know he does not. God takes all sin seriously, and we are glad for that when we long for the judgment of the monsters of history. But we often dislike the fact that God takes sin just as seriously when he evaluates the sins of our friends who do not know Christ.

But that is what Scripture teaches, and that is what we must believe. Biblical teaching on hell is by no means popular right now. As a result, it is easier to downplay this doctrine. After all, the doctrine of hell repels people in our society, even leading them to think that Christians are narrow-minded and intolerant. In a sense, hell stands for everything that contemporary culture rejects—that God's love is not sentimental but is just, that humans are wicked by nature and choice, that Jesus is the only Savior of the world, that faith in Christ is the only way to receive God's forgiveness, and that sin will ultimately be punished, either through Christ's substitutionary work or in hell. Consequently, to believe in and speak of hell today is to invite widespread opposition.

But what is the alternative? Not to embrace or speak of hell? No, that is not an option for Christians, because God's Word clearly teaches the reality of hell. Every New Testament author speaks of the reality of the future punishment of the wicked.[11] And the Lord Jesus himself stands out as hell's chief defender. We who call Jesus "Lord" do not have the option of rejecting or neglecting a doctrine so explicit in Scripture and so emphatic in our Lord's teachings. As Sinclair Ferguson points out:

> Hell is at the end of the day the darkness outside; dense like a black hole, it is the place of cosmic waste. Who can contemplate this for long? Who, indeed, is sufficient for these things? The question is surely rhetorical. None of us is sufficient. But our sufficiency is to be found in Christ, the Savior, the perfect Man, the Redeemer, the Judge. We must constantly remind ourselves that it is the Savior who spoke clearly of the dark side of eternity. To be faithful to him, so must we.[12]

The Christian Worldview and Hell

Although hell is not as central to the Christian worldview as God, sin, and Jesus' saving work are, it is clearly taught in the Word of God and is linked to these core tenets of the faith.[13] To downplay or reject hell usually means to err in other important beliefs also. Reworking hell is often an early indicator that other things have been redefined. Christian beliefs hang together. They are like threads that interweave. For example, only when we recognize God's holiness will we know the horror of sin. Only when we become aware of the awfulness of our sin will we know the dreadfulness of hell and what it cost Jesus to save us. Only when we grapple with the punishment of hell, the cost of Christ's atoning death, and the inestimable joy of heaven can we begin to grasp God's amazing grace.

God and Hell

Belief in hell emerges from a biblical understanding of God. Those who reject the historic doctrine of hell often argue against it because they view it as inconsistent with God's love and mercy. But while God's love is certainly central in Scripture, it is not all there is to God. John Piper reminds, "The statement 'God is love' does not imply that God relates to individuals only in terms of love."[14] David Wells aptly warns, "Of course the Bible tells us that God is love, but the Christians of modernity seem to think that this constitutes an adequate theology in itself, that God is fundamentally if not exclusively love."[15] Wells also notes the tendency in contemporary evangelicalism to soften the doctrine of God:

> We have turned to a God that we can use rather than to a God we must obey; we have turned to a God who will fulfill our needs rather than to a God before whom we must surrender our rights to ourselves. . . . And so we transform the God of mercy into a God who is at our mercy.

> We imagine that he is benign . . . and if the sunshine
> of his benign grace fails to warm us as we expect, if he
> fails to shower prosperity and success on us, we will
> find ourselves unable to believe in him anymore. . . .
> It is our fallenness fleshed out in our modernity that
> makes God smooth, that imagines he will accommodate
> our instincts, shabby and self-centered as they so often
> are, because he is love. . . . We need to recover a sense
> of God's transcendence.[16]

Make no mistake: God's love is far greater than we can
conceive (Ps. 103:11; Eph. 3:19). But we also need to remember, and to remind those in our culture, that God's love is not
sentimentality. Our loving God is also just, holy, good, and,
because we rebel against him, wrathful. God's love should
not be viewed as suggesting that he cannot bear to see justice
executed—as if punishing the wicked hurts him more than
it hurts them. Jonathan Edwards offers insight:

> It is an unreasonable and unscriptural notion of the
> mercy of God that He is merciful in such a sense that
> He cannot bear that penal justice should be executed.
> This is to conceive of the mercy of God as a passion
> to which His nature is so subject that God is liable to
> be moved, affected, and overcome by seeing a crea-
> ture in misery so that He cannot bear to see justice
> executed. . . . The Scriptures everywhere present the
> mercy of God as free and sovereign, and not that the
> exercises of it are necessary.[17]

Because of the unity of God, all attempts to separate his
love from his justice should be rejected. God's love does not
drive his justice. The implementation of God's justice does

not undermine his love. God's love and justice cohere, as do all his other attributes. John Frame explains this historic understanding of God:

> None of his attributes can be removed from him, and no new attribute can be added to him. Not one attribute exists without the others. So each attribute has divine attributes; each is qualified by the others. God's wisdom is an eternal wisdom; his goodness is a wise goodness and a just goodness. . . . The essential attributes of God are "perspectival." That is, each of them describes everything that God is, from a different perspective. In one sense, any attribute may be taken as central, and the others seen in relation to it. But in that sense, the doctrine of God has many centers, not just one.[18]

Approaching God's attributes in this way is much wiser because we view the doctrine of God according to the whole of Scripture, and in so doing we hold these truths about God in proper proportion, refusing to exalt any one attribute of God in such a way as to undercut the others.

The biblical portrait of God is that he does not delight in people going to hell and has gone to great lengths to offer forgiveness—"he gave his only Son," who "humbled himself by becoming obedient to the point of death, even death on a cross" (John 3:16; Phil. 2:8). But Scripture also paints the picture of a holy and just God "who will by no means clear the guilty" and has in store "the day of wrath when God's righteous judgment will be revealed" (Ex. 34:7; Rom. 2:5).

Humanity, Sin, and Hell

Hell is also connected to a biblical understanding of humanity and sin. Hell reminds us that *being human comes with awesome privileges and responsibilities.* To choose *sin* rather than *God* is a high crime indeed. While hell is in a sense an awful reality, sin is actually the ultimate horror of God's universe. Hell is the punishment, but sin is the crime. Which is worse, murder or the life sentence? Obviously, the crime is worse than the punishment. The Bible is clear: sin is inherently *against God*, who is infinite in all his perfections. Sin, then, is an infinite evil and merits endless punishment. So from the perspective of human rebellion against our Maker, hell is not a horror in God's universe, but a demonstration of final and decisive justice in a universe marred by the horror of sin.

Too often we underestimate how horrible sin really is. What would be the best way to evaluate the horror of murder? Would it be to survey hundreds of murderers on death row to ask their opinions on the proper extent of their punishment? Of course not. On the whole, the penalty would be minimized by them. Why? Because they are the offenders, not the offended parties. It would be a much better approach to interview hundreds of mothers, fathers, wives, husbands, friends, sons, and daughters of the murder victims. They would be able to provide a much more reliable account of the horror of murder. They would also be able to demonstrate a better understanding of its corresponding penalty. Why? Because they are the ones affected by this evil.

In the same way, we fallen humans tend to underestimate the sinfulness of sin. We have a propensity to view our sins as accidents, blunders, or mistakes. But unless sin is viewed in light of the holiness of God, it will never be seen as the evil, odious, and damnable thing that it really is (see also Isa. 6). We offenders fail to measure it correctly. Only the all-holy and offended God knows the full extent of the sinfulness of sin.

Jesus and Hell

Hell is also linked to truths concerning Jesus. Jesus is not only the chief teacher about hell, but also the only Savior from it. Fully divine and fully human, Jesus the Mediator died on the cross as the only substitute for our sin. He bore the infinite penalty of sin for every believer. But those who fail to come to Christ in faith and repentance will have to pay that penalty themselves in endless punishment.

There are only two ways to measure how much God hates sin. One is by looking at the cross, where Christ paid for the sin of all who would ever believe in him. The other is by looking at hell, where all who fail to trust Christ pay for their own sins. To minimize hell, therefore, is to minimize the cross. To begin to realize the horror of hell is to begin to understand the infinite value of Christ's death.

On the cross, Jesus dies as a substitute for our sins and drinks the cup of divine wrath (Matt. 26:42; Rom. 3:25–26; 1 Peter 3:18). On the cross, Jesus offers himself as a sacrifice for our sins in death (see also Heb. 9–10). On the cross, Jesus experiences separation from his Father's fellowship as he cries, "My God, my God, why have you forsaken me?" (Matt. 27:46). Sinclair Ferguson's comments are insightful:

> It is as characteristic of Jesus' teaching to warn against the prospect of hell as it is for him to describe the high privileges of heaven. For him, at least, hell is just as real as heaven. In addition, if we take seriously the significance of his death on the cross as a sacrifice of atonement (Rom. 3:25 NIV), what, short of the reality of hell, explains the necessity for and nature of his sufferings? It would be folly to think that all he went through was merely exemplary, or for that matter unnecessary. The cry of dereliction is an enigma

whose only solution is Christ's enduring of hell—his separation from and sense of the absence of God in order to save us from it. . . .

Here, then, on the cross, is all that makes hell into hell: darkness, pain, isolation, sin-bearing, divine judgment, curse, alienation, utter darkness, separation from God. If we need to be convinced of the reality of hell, all we need to do is to consider the cross. It is all there. . . .

Sin against an eternal Person brings eternal judgment; that eternal judgment was accepted, received, and experienced by Christ as one who is an eternal Person capable of bearing it until he has exhausted it in death and rises again in the new order of the Last Man.

Why is this apparent digression from the topic of hell important? Because it underlines hell's reality—Jesus experienced it. It is at the same time the clearest indication of hell's awfulness. Yet, simultaneously and gloriously, it is the divine provision to enable us to escape. And it is in this context that preaching on hell belongs to the preaching of the gospel. When a man understands that this is what the death of Christ means, when this grips his soul, he will begin to find the apostolic model of preaching reduplicated in his own ministry.[19]

Heaven and Hell

Scripture depicts heaven and hell as parallel final destinies.

And many of those who sleep in the dust of the earth shall awake, some to everlasting life, and some to shame and everlasting contempt. (Dan. 12:2)

And these will go away into eternal punishment, but the righteous into eternal life. (Matt. 25:46)

Do not marvel at this, for an hour is coming when all who are in the tombs will hear his voice and come out, those who have done good to the resurrection of life, and those who have done evil to the resurrection of judgment. (John 5:28–29)

Scripture puts heaven and hell side by side. Every human being will exist forever in one or the other. Heaven and hell must be understood as alternative destinies. That means that the joys of heaven shed light on the torments of hell. And heaven's glories are properly appreciated only against hell's agonies. The Bible paints at least six pictures of heaven.

First, heaven is the renewal of creation. It is God's delivering his good creation from the curse of sin (Rom. 8:19–22). Resurrected believers will live forever under the new heavens and on the new earth (Isa. 66:22; 2 Peter 3:10–13; Rev. 21–22). By contrast, lost human beings will be banished from the city of God and will suffer forever in the lake of fire (Rev. 20:15; 21:8; 22:15).

Second, heaven is the final stage of the kingdom of God. The struggles of the present life will be past when, by God's grace, saved human beings exercise dominion with Christ. Human life will flourish and human culture will thrive in the city of God (Heb. 2:5–10; Rev. 21:24–26). Jesus will return, deliver his people, and bring the final installment of his kingdom (Rev. 11:15). But the wicked will not inherit the kingdom of God. Instead King Jesus will condemn them to "eternal punishment" (Matt. 25:46), even "the eternal fire prepared for the devil and his angels" (Matt. 25:41; see also Rev. 20:10, 15).

Third, heaven is the everlasting rest of God's people. There will be no more sin and strife in the lives of individuals, families, and nations when the saints find their fulfillment eagerly serving Jesus in the perpetual Sabbath-rest of the new creation (Heb. 4:9–11; Rev. 14:13). And the wicked? "The smoke of their torment goes up forever and ever, and they have no rest, day or night" (Rev. 14:11).

Fourth, heaven is being in the gracious presence of God forever. In ourselves we would fear to stand before our Maker; but because of the finished and perfect work of Christ, when he returns we will delight in his presence. Heaven and earth will be one in that day as God himself dwells in the midst of his people as never before (Ps. 16:11; Rev. 21:3, 22). But the unbelieving "will suffer the punishment of eternal destruction, away from the presence of the Lord and from the glory of his might" (2 Thess. 1:9).

Fifth, heaven is the final seeing of God that fills the beholders with joy. When we see Christ, we will be like him because our sight will be perfected (1 John 3:2–3). We will "see his face" (Rev. 22:4). While redeemed human beings will rejoice to see their gracious God, the unsaved will be in outer darkness, where "there will be weeping and gnashing of teeth" (Matt. 8:12; 13:42, 50; 22:13; 24:51; 25:30; Luke 13:28).

Sixth, heaven is our shining in glory forever. Our bodies will be raised in glory and our whole beings will be glorified. Not only will we behold God's glory, we will be transformed by it so that we actually partake of his glory. The glory of the Trinity will flood the new heavens and new earth forever (1 Cor. 15:43; 1 Peter 5:1; Rev. 21:10–11, 19–26). By contrast, the wicked will be raised and fitted for "shame and everlasting contempt" (Dan. 12:2), the suffering of everlasting destruction in body and soul (Matt. 10:28).

All have sinned and deserve hell, but God gives heaven to all who have trusted Christ! When viewed as alternatives, heaven looks even more glorious and hell even more dreadful.

The Church's Mission and Hell

Thinking about hell also moves us to ask God to fill our hearts with compassion for the lost. Romans 9 is a theologically rich portion of Scripture, where Paul traverses some of the most difficult doctrinal terrain: God's sovereignty and human responsibility, the relationship of Israel and the Gentiles, and an overall approach to salvation history. Yet at the beginning and the end of this chapter, Paul shows what it means to have a burden for the lost. Paul expresses his personal wish that he could go to hell in place of his countrymen, the Jews. "I have great sorrow and unceasing anguish in my heart. For I could wish that I myself were accursed and cut off from Christ for the sake of my brothers, my kinsmen according to the flesh. They are Israelites" (Rom. 9:2–4). His heart is heavy because he knows that many of them are heading for God's wrath. He begins the very next chapter deeply longing and praying that they would trust Christ: "Brothers, my heart's desire and prayer to God for them [his fellow Jews] is that they may be saved" (Rom. 10:1). John Piper addresses this passionately:

> Should not our heart feel what Paul felt? Should we not grieve over the misery of the lost—especially over our kinsmen? Should we not have the same desire for their salvation that Paul had? Should we not look upon the people at our workplaces with a mixture of sorrow for their condition and longing for their conversion? Can we claim to be Biblical Christians if, day in and day out, we work and eat and laugh with unbelievers and feel none of these things?[20]

That people go to hell is a tragedy. It is tragic that sin entered the world through Adam. It is tragic that humans continue to rebel against God. And it is tragic that sinners still reject Jesus as Lord and Savior. In this sense, the horror of hell should bother us. Even more, the suffering of those in hell should break our hearts—not only because of the dreadfulness of the punishment in hell, but especially because of the awfulness of sin, the crime that demanded such a penalty. But the problem is not hell, and the problem is not God. Sin is the problem, and it is what should repulse us. Sinclair Ferguson captures our need for such a burden:

> When Robert M'Cheyne met his dearest friend Andrew Bonar one Monday and enquired what Bonar had preached on the previous day, only to receive the answer "Hell," he asked: "Did you preach it with tears?" That we cannot do until we have come to recognize our own great need of grace to save us from the wrath to come, the terrible nature of that judgment, the provision that God has made for us in Christ, and the calling he has given us to take the gospel to every creature in the name of the One who did not come into the world to condemn it, but to save it.[21]

Belief in hell should lead us to share the gospel. Most of us know people who if they died today would spend eternity in hell. We work with them, live next door to them, and go fishing with them. We may even live in the same house with them. We know that they will not make it to heaven apart from having faith in Christ. And they will not trust Christ unless they hear and believe. And they will not know the gospel unless a Christian shares it with them. We lament that today some evangelical Christians teach inclusivism, the view that it is possible for people to be saved by Jesus without believing the gospel. We have coedited a book that opposes this idea and defends the view that anyone who would be saved must trust Christ as Lord and Savior.[22] Paul makes this clear in Romans 10:13–15, 17:

For "everyone who calls on the name of the Lord will be saved."

But how are they to call on him in whom they have not believed? And how are they to believe in him of whom they have never heard? And how are they to hear without someone preaching? And how are they to preach unless they are sent? . . . So faith comes from hearing, and hearing through the word of Christ.

May our earnestness reflect that of Charles Haddon Spurgeon. He urges unbelievers:

To be laughed at is no great hardship for me. I can delight in scoffs and jeers . . . but that you should turn from your own mercy, this is my sorrow. Spit on me, but, oh, repent! Laugh at me, but, oh, believe in my Master! Make my body as the dirt in the streets, but do not damn your own souls.

He also passionately exhorts the church:

If sinners be damned, at least let them leap to hell over our bodies. And if they perish, let them perish with our arms about their knees, imploring them to stay. If hell must be filled, at least let it be filled in the teeth of our exertions, and let not one person go there unwarned and unprayed for.

In addition, he instructs:

The Holy Spirit will move them by first moving you. If you can rest without their being saved, they will rest, too. But if you are filled with an agony for them, if you cannot bear that they are lost, you will soon find that they are uneasy, too.[23]

We close with a prayer for ourselves and our readers: Lord, give us courage to stand on your truth even when it is unpopular. Remind us, Lord, that hell is important and holds a key place in the Christian worldview. Lord Jesus, thank you for experiencing hell for us on the cross. Thank you, Lord, for giving us heaven when we deserve hell. Lord, help us to share the gospel with our friends, family, neighbors, and coworkers. O Lord, give us the passion to make your name known to the ends of the earth!

FOR FURTHER READING

Carson, Donald A. *The Gagging of God: Christianity Confronts Pluralism*. Grand Rapids: Zondervan, 1996, pp. 491–536.

Davies, Eryl. *An Angry God? What the Bible Says about Wrath, Final Judgment, and Hell*. Bridgend, UK: Evangelical Press of Wales, 1991.

Dixon, Larry. *The Other Side of the Good News: Confronting the Contemporary Challenges to Jesus' Teaching on Hell*. Fearn, Ross-shire, UK: Christian Focus, 2003.

Fudge, Edward William, and Robert A. Peterson. *Two Views of Hell: A Biblical and Theological Dialogue*. Downers Grove, IL: InterVarsity, 2000.

Milne, Bruce. *The Message of Heaven and Hell: Grace and Destiny*. The Bible Speaks Today. Downers Grove, IL: InterVarsity, 2002.

Morgan, Christopher W. *Jonathan Edwards and Hell*. Fearn, Ross-shire, UK: Christian Focus, 2004.

Morgan, Christopher W., and Robert A. Peterson, eds. *Hell under Fire: Modern Scholarship Reinvents Eternal Punishment*. Grand Rapids: Zondervan, 2004.

———. *Faith Comes by Hearing: A Response to Inclusivism*. Downers Grove, IL: InterVarsity, 2008.

Morris, Leon. *The Biblical Doctrine of Judgment*. Grand Rapids: Eerdmans, 1960.

Peterson, Robert A. *Hell on Trial: The Case for Eternal Punishment*. Phillipsburg, NJ: P&R Publishing, 1995.

Shedd, William G. T. *The Doctrine of Endless Punishment*. New York: Charles Scribner's Sons, 1886. Reprint, Minneapolis: Klock & Klock, 1980.

NOTES

1 K. Connie Kang, "Next Stop, the Pearly Gates . . . or Hell?" *Los Angeles Times*, October 24, 2003.

2 Jeffrey L. Sheler, "Hell's Sober Comeback," *U.S. News & World Report*, March 25, 1991, 56–63.

3 Timothy J. Keller, *The Reason for God: Belief in an Age of Skepticism* (New York: Dutton, 2008), 68–83.

4 For a careful case for the necessity of hearing and believing the gospel for salvation, see Christopher W. Morgan and Robert A. Peterson, eds., *Faith Comes by Hearing: A Response to Inclusivism* (Downers Grove, IL: InterVarsity, 2008).

5 Douglas J. Moo, "Paul on Hell," in *Hell under Fire: Modern Scholarship Reinvents Eternal Punishment*, ed. Christopher W. Morgan and Robert A. Peterson (Grand Rapids: Zondervan, 2004), 105.

6 Examples are Tertullian, Augustine, Thomas Aquinas, Martin Luther, John Calvin, and Jonathan Edwards. See Robert A. Peterson, *Hell on Trial: The Case for Eternal Punishment* (Phillipsburg, NJ: P&R Publishing, 1995), 97–138.

7 For a defense of annihilationism and a critique of it, see Edward William Fudge and Robert A. Peterson, *Two Views of Hell: A Biblical and Theological Dialogue* (Downers Grove, IL: InterVarsity, 2000).

8 Peterson, *Hell on Trial*, 21–96, 139–202; Christopher W. Morgan, "Annihilationism: Will the Unsaved Be Punished Forever?" in Morgan and Peterson, *Hell under Fire*, 195–218; Christopher W. Morgan, *Jonathan Edwards and Hell* (Fearn, Ross-shire, UK: Christian Focus, 2004).

9 The adjective *eternal* means "age-long," with the context determining the length of the "age." The age to come is determined by the life of God himself and thus is never-ending. See Peterson, *Hell on Trial*, 34–36.

10 J. I. Packer, "Evangelicals and the Way of Salvation," in *Evangelical Affirmations*, ed. Kenneth S. Kantzer and Carl F. H. Henry (Grand Rapids: Zondervan, 1990), 117.

11 Christopher W. Morgan, "Biblical Theology: Three Pictures of Hell," in Morgan and Peterson, *Hell under Fire*, 135–51.

12 Sinclair B. Ferguson, "Pastoral Theology: The Preacher and Hell," in Morgan and Peterson, *Hell under Fire*, 237.

13 See Christopher W. Morgan and Robert A. Peterson, "Conclusion,"
    in Morgan and Peterson, *Hell under Fire*, 239–40.

14 John Piper, "How Does a Sovereign God Love?" *Reformed Journal*
    2 (April 1983): 11.

15 David F. Wells, *God in the Wasteland: The Reality of Truth in a World of
    Fading Dreams* (Grand Rapids: Eerdmans, 1994), 135.

16 Ibid., 114–16.

17 Jonathan Edwards, "The Eternity of Hell Torments," in *The Wrath of
    Almighty God: Jonathan Edwards on God's Judgment against Sinners*,
    ed. Don Kistler (Morgan, PA: Soli Deo Gloria, 1996), 339–40.

18 John M. Frame, *No Other God: A Response to Open Theism* (Phillipsburg,
    NJ: P&R Publishing, 2001), 52.

19 Ferguson, "Pastoral Theology," 226, 231, 232.

20 John Piper, "My Heart's Desire: That They May Be Saved," sermon
    preached on January 5, 1986, available at http://www.desiringgod
    .org/ResourceLibrary/Sermons/ByScripture/10/473_My_Hearts
    _Desire_That_They_Might_Be_Saved.

21 Ferguson, "Pastoral Theology," 234.

22 Morgan and Peterson, *Faith Comes by Hearing*.

23 Charles Haddon Spurgeon, *Spurgeon at His Best*, ed. Tom Carter (Grand
    Rapids: Baker, 1991), 67–68.